COACHING 101

Handbook

Robert E. Logan
and Gary B. Reinecke

COACHING 101 HANDBOOK

By Robert E. Logan and Gary B. Reinecke

Cover design by: Michelle Coe of BlueSkyPhoenix LLC

Published by Logan Leadership

Visit us at http://loganleadership.com

ISBN 10: 1-944955-49-6

ISBN 13: 978-1-944955-49-6

Printed in the United States of America

FOREWORD

As I look back on the 15 years since this handbook was first published, the main attribute I am struck by is its durability. The work Gary Reinecke and I did with Dr. Charles Ridley on the international qualitative research project to determine coaching competencies, micro-skills and outcomes was a pioneering work yielding robust results that have stood the test of time.

The principles are now proven through the training of thousands of coaches throughout the world. To date, *Coaching 101 Handbook* has been translated into Spanish, German, Russian, Portuguese, Italian, and French. As a part of a global coach training process, it's proven to be a very powerful tool.

Over the years, coaching has grown and increasingly impacted churches and ministries. Its principles have been applied to increase the effectiveness of making disciples and raising leaders. Perhaps the reason it's been so powerful is because it was extracted from biblical principles. It's about coming alongside to help, just as Barnabas came alongside Paul, and then Paul came alongside Timothy and others, empowering them for effective ministry. It's about listening to the Holy Spirit and respecting others enough to believe that they too can listen to the Holy Spirit and live in obedience to what they're hearing.

I look forward to seeing God at work as you use this resource to increase your coaching skills for coming alongside others and helping release their fullest potential for ministry expansion and multiplication. Those kinds of intentional coaching relationships will foster personal growth as well as increasing fruitful results for the Kingdom of God. May God continue to work through the timelessness of these materials, relevant 15 years later and for years to come.

Blessings,

Robert E. Logan

ACKNOWLEDGMENTS

From Bob

Dr. Charles Ridley mentored us through an extensive qualitative research project to determine the coaching outcomes and process. We are grateful for his wisdom and encouragement throughout the journey.

Jeannette Buller helped with the development of reflection and coaching questions. Her contributions to the design and framework of the handbook greatly enhanced the usefulness.

Tara Miller assisted with writing and editing.

Janet, my wife, continues to encourage and support me. Thank you for your godly example that challenges me to grow in my relationship with God.

From Gary

Dr. Dallas and Nancy Demmitt – For their initial contributions in the analysis of the coaching process. We are grateful for your partnership.

For the many coaches we interviewed in our research – Here are but a few of those who gave selflessly of their time: Jeannette Buller, Neil Cole, Paul Kaak, Michael Ledner, Tom Nebel, Gayle Parker, Ray Vialpando.

Gina – For your friendship, patience and love. You have coached me to become a better husband and father.

Dad – You have helped me learn about life and leadership. Thank you for being a godly example and mentor.

Joel & Zoe – You helped me see the light side when things got serious. May God bless you as you grow in His love.

TABLE OF CONTENTS

HOW TO USE THIS HANDBOOK

The *Coaching 101 Handbook* supplements the material in *Coaching 101* for those who want to go deeper and put more focused energy into improving their coaching skills. The handbook fleshes out key issues in coaching with summaries, checklists, worksheets, reflection questions, and more. Everything you need to apply the powerful principles of *Coaching 101* is right here.

A companion volume to *Coaching 101*, the *Coaching 101 Handbook* outlines and summarizes the main points of the book so you can quickly and easily see the structure of a coaching relationship and the actions needed at each stage. Divided into five sections—one for each of the five phases of the coaching relationship—each part includes:

- An overview of this phase of the coaching relationship, including its purpose and significance
- 4 to 7 key actions that need to be accomplished during this phase of the coaching process
- Reflection questions for each key action to help you personalize the material and apply some of the most crucial coaching skills
- Helpful worksheets you can give to those you are coaching or use during coaching appointments
- A final checklist for each of the key actions
- Coaching questions you can ask those you are coaching

The *Coaching 101 Handbook* will walk you step by step through the material, outlining the major issues and points to consider in each phase of the coaching relationship and stopping along the way to ask reflection questions. Use these questions to evaluate your current situation: What do you do well? Where do you need to grow? What steps could you take to improve?

For example, the question "What strategies do you employ to avoid simply 'telling' people your solutions?" can help you think through when you 'tell', when you don't, what makes the difference, what works for you, and how you can avoid 'telling' in the future. Don't skip over giving concrete examples from your own life and ministry—it will yield powerful dividends.

You will also find the coaching questions immediately applicable. You can use these with people you are coaching to isolate and examine key issues in each stage of the relationship. If you pinpoint a problem area in assessing the compatibility of a coaching relationship, four questions are available for you to use. By asking, "What do we need to discuss in order to work together well?" and listening to the answer, you will begin to better understand how to address the issue with this particular person.

The coaching journal at the end of the handbook provides a place for you to track your development as a coach. Here you can record key insights, action plans and powerful questions for future use. Intentionalize your personal development by periodically setting aside time to reflect and mine the wisdom from your coaching experience.

You are free to photocopy the worksheets included in this handbook for exclusive use within one local church. Some, such as the coaching log and the coaching agreement, are indispensable in creating an effective structure for the relationship. Others, such as "What God has called you to do?" and "Balancing personal roles and priorities," can be given to those you are coaching to help them sort through vision and priorities at the appropriate stages of the coaching relationship.

By taking the time to study these pages, you can improve your coaching skills and begin to master new ones. The people you coach will see the difference.

OVERVIEW

WHAT IS COACHING?

- Coaches come alongside to help — like Barnabas. By encouraging and challenging others, Barnabas empowered them for ministry. He may not have been in the starring role, but without him many others would not have been able to accomplish the great things for God that they did.

- The goal of coaching is to help someone succeed.

- What is success? It's finding out what God wants you to do and doing it. Given that definition, success will necessarily look different on different people.

- Each person needs to discover for themselves what it is that God wants them to do. Coaches aid that process, but they don't direct it. Coaching is not about telling others what to do; it's about helping them discover it for themselves.

> Coaching is the process of coming alongside a person or team to help them discover God's agenda for their life and ministry, and then cooperating with the Holy Spirit to see that agenda become a reality.

WHAT IS THE PROCESS OF COACHING?

- Every journey requires a good map. Coaching is no different. Coaches need an easy framework that helps them understand what needs to be accomplished in the coaching process. Many coaching models are not comprehensive; those that are comprehensive are not simple.

- The coaching process consists of five basic phases. Coaching relationships need to move through each phase and accomplish the necessary outcomes in order to be optimally effective.

Coaching Process
Relate – Establish coaching relationship and agenda
Reflect – Discover and explore key issues
Refocus – Determine priorities and action steps
Resource – Provide support and encouragement
Review – Evaluate, celebrate, and revise plans

Relate: Establish coaching relationship and agenda

Coaching at its core is about qualities like trust, connection, support, and understanding. Sometimes coaches are tempted to skip over the relate stage in hopes of getting to the heart of things faster and accomplishing more. Don't—that strategy will backfire. Coaching that leaves out the relational element may move through agenda items faster, but will ultimately be ineffective. Ninety percent of the time the people who have the deepest impact on our lives are those we know on a personal level, those who have taken the time to invest in developing a relationship with us. Forming a trusting, growing relationship will exponentially increase the significance and effectiveness of your coaching.

Reflect: Discover and explore key issues

The reflection process helps us figure out where we are. When people get lost in a shopping mall, most will go to a directory and look for the "you are here" sign. You cannot take any steps toward a goal unless you first know where you are starting from. Some point of reference is needed. In a coaching relationship, the reflect stage helps people figure out where they are in their lives and ministries and identify the most significant issues to address.

Refocus: Determine priorities and action steps

After we've figured out where we are, the next step in the process is to ask, "Where do we want to go from here?" This is the task of the refocus stage— gaining a sense of direction and forward movement. In order to do this, we need long-range vision to see where God wants us to go in the future and short-range vision to see the individual steps it will take to get there. Effective action planning addresses the questions of who, what, where, when, and how.

Resource: Provide support and encouragement

Once we have discovered where we are and where we want to go, the next question is, "What do we need?" Answering this question is the primary task of the resource stage. Christian leaders often spend enormous amounts of time reinventing the wheel when many quality resources already exist that can save time, money, and energy. A good coach guides people in the direction of those resources that will be most useful to them given where they are and where they want to go.

Review: Evaluate, celebrate, and revise plans

The review stage allows us to look back over our progress and ask, "What has been accomplished?" Never underestimate the power of taking the time to look back over past accomplishments and celebrate them. That process can provide both a sense of satisfaction over a job well done and much-needed encouragement for the road ahead. The evaluation process also maximizes learning and provides opportunities to make mid-course corrections.

POWERFUL COACHING QUESTIONS

RELATE

- How are you doing?
- Where are you now?
- How can I be praying for you?
- What do you want to address?
- How can we work together?

REFLECT

- What can we celebrate?
- What's really important?
- What obstacles are you facing?
- Where do you want to go?
- How committed are you?

REFOCUS

- What do you want to accomplish?
- What are possible ways to get there?
- Which path will you choose?
- What will you do? (who, what, where, when, how)
- How will you measure your progress?

RESOURCE

- What resources do you already have?
- What resources will you need to accomplish your goals? (people, finances, knowledge, etc.)
- What resources are missing?
- Where will you find the resources you need?
- What can I do to support you?

REVIEW

- What's working?
- What's not working?
- What are you learning?
- What needs to change?
- What further training would be helpful?
- What's next in our coaching relationship?

NOTES

RELATE

ESTABLISH THE COACHING RELATIONSHIP AND AGENDA

Always remember that change is most often inspired by relationship. Proper attention to the coaching relationship is essential. Try beginning and ending each appointment with a relational component to instill trust, facilitate learning, and enhance results.

The relate phase of the coaching process focuses on the coaching relationship. Developing the relational bond is vital to every coaching relationship; it sets the stage for the subsequent phases.

The parameters you set during this phase will determine the course of the future coaching relationship. During this phase the coach is CONNECTING on several fronts, namely the personal, spiritual, and philosophical. Guidelines for the coaching relationship must be clarified before advancing to the next phase.

Key actions in the RELATE phase:

Coaching relationship and process defined
Compatibility of coach and leader assessed
Rapport and mutual respect established
Trusting relationship begun
Coaching agenda and guidelines determined

COACHING RELATIONSHIP AND PROCESS DEFINED

- As you define the coaching relationship, pay attention to the hopes and expectations that you personally bring to the table. Determine which ones are non-negotiable and which ones you can meet another way.
- Recognize what is important to you in a coaching relationship. Values such as directness, sensitivity, and being on time should be addressed up front if these are important to you. Taking the time to arrive at a mutual understanding is well worth it.

Reflection Questions

1. What kinds of coaching opportunities do you want to pursue? Consider your gifts, calling, and experience.
2. What do you value in a coaching relationship?
3. What coaching environments and methods have been most fruitful for you personally and for those you coach?
4. What specific agreements will guide your coaching relationships?

COMPATBILITY OF COACH AND LEADER ASSESSED

- Determining compatibility in your vision, values, philosophy of ministry, behavioral styles, etc. is critical to a healthy coaching relationship. Most mistakes that occur in the relate phase begin here. Making assumptions based on little information, wrong information, or no information can cause conflict.

- Behavioral styles are particularly important keys to an effective coaching relationship. Knowing your behavioral style and the style of the other person will begin to clarify what adjustments need to be made.

- Two factors will determine your effectiveness in making those adjustments. The first is your flexibility, or your willingness to change. The second is your versatility, or your ability to change. When both factors come together effectiveness increases.

- An accurate assessment of behavioral styles can be gained by taking an inventory such as the Personal Profile System 2800 (DiSC) Inventory. Inventories such as these are best administered early in the coaching process. During the first coaching session, discuss ways to maximize the fruitfulness of your coaching relationship given each other's behavioral style.

- Laying the groundwork for strong communication now will greatly enhance the coaching process.

Reflection Questions

1. How have you adjusted your behavioral style in order to work more effectively with another person or group? Give 2-3 examples.

2. How could your behavioral tendencies cause tension in those you coach?

3. What changes could you make that will increase your flexibility and effectiveness?

4. How willing are you to make these adjustments?

5. What compatibility issues do you consider nonnegotiable?

RAPPORT AND MUTUAL RESPECT ESTABLISHED

- Beginning with the intake session, excellent coaches invest in the relationship. Harmony, agreement, consideration, honor, and esteem are important ingredients to a healthy coaching relationship. Time and energy invested at this stage will pay huge dividends later.
- Make a considerable investment in both the personal and ministry development of the leader. Try to discover common ground and find ways to give affirmation. Be sure to notice and mention the contributions they are making to you personally. Make it a point to discuss the best ways for communication to take place.

Reflection Questions

1. How can I find common ground with the people I am coaching?

2. How can I affirm the leaders I am coaching?

3. How are you growing through your coaching relationships?

TRUSTING RELATIONSHIP BEGUN

- Confidentiality is a foundational element leading to trust. Where trust is lacking, the relationship quickly digresses and loses momentum, sacrificing that sense of destiny. However, when trust is established, the relationship builds momentum, the rate of progress increases, and the number of accomplishments grow exponentially.

- Identify ways you can establish trust. Identify the obstacles hindering a trusting relationship and determine ways to address those. Ask yourself what relational risks you and the leader are taking in order to enter into the coaching relationship. Consider also the physical location for your meetings and determine how conducive they are to building trust.

Reflection Questions

1. Think about a time when you have experienced a breach of confidentiality. What were the ramifications?

2. How have you established trust in relationships? What else could you do?

RELATE

COACHING AGENDA AND GUIDELINES DETERMINED

- A coaching agreement is critical to a healthy coaching relationship. An agreement clarifies things like purpose, goals, expectations, regularity, venue, communication, and evaluation.

- A written document can serve as a helpful reference point to remind you and the leader of the commitments made and the process you will follow.

Reflection Questions

1. What will be the focus of this coaching relationship?

2. What specific objectives do you want to accomplish by working together?

3. What commitments will we make? (e.g. confidentiality, follow through, use of coaching tools for preparation, etc.)

Logistical questions

- How often will we meet?
- Where and how will we meet?
- How long will each coaching meeting last?
- What expenses are involved?
- When and how will we evaluate our effectiveness?

SAMPLE COACHING AGREEMENT

Below is a sample coaching agreement between a lay coach and a new small group leader who would like help getting his group started. You can adapt this agreement to fit your context, goals, and preferred guidelines.

- **Agenda and goals:** The focus of the coaching relationship is to help launch a new small group. Initial goals include the recruitment of apprentices, the recruitment of group members, the establishment of healthy group norms, and learning more effective ways of facilitating group discussions.

- **Meetings:** We'll meet twice a month for the first two months as the group is being formed, then once a month after that. Meetings will take place on Thursdays over the lunch hour at a restaurant partway between our offices and will last for 45 minutes.

- **Additional contact:** If questions arise, I am available via email and phone.

- **Commitments and expectations:**
    - Be on time for appointments.
    - Call if you need to cancel or reschedule.
    - Commit to addressing the agreed upon issues and following through on assignments. All goals and assignments will be set down in writing via online coaching to avoid miscommunication and to ensure accountability.
    - Confidentiality will be maintained except where permission is expressly granted or where disclosures affect the ability to continue serving in a ministry capacity.

- **Length of coaching commitment:** We'll begin coaching March 1 and work together for three months. At that point, we'll evaluate the effectiveness of the coaching relationship and the present situation and make a decision as to whether it would be beneficial to continue for another three month period.

Reference: Logan, Robert E. and Carlton, Sherilyn. Coaching 101, page 121.

COACHING AGREEMENT

Leader: ______________________ Date: __________

Coach: ______________________

Coaching focus: ______________________

Specific objectives: ______________________

Mutual commitments: ______________________

Logistics (duration, frequency, expenses, etc): ______________________

Evaluation date(s): ______________________

COACHING LOG

Leader: ______________________ Date: __________

Coach: ______________________

Agenda: ______________________

Progress: ______________________

Challenges: ______________________

Prayer: ______________________

COACHING LOG

Key Issues
(Use this to organize your Action Plans)

Action Plans	Item	Completion Date

Next Appointment Date ________ Time: ________ am/pm Time Zone: ________

Notes

POWERFUL QUESTIONS

Relate Checklist

Coaching relationship and process defined

- Where are you now?
- What's important to you in a coaching relationship?
- What do you want to address?
- How can we work together?
- What pitfalls do you want to avoid?

Compatibility of coach and leader assessed

- What prompted you to seek a coaching relationship with me?
- What can I do (or not do) that will help you get the most out of our coaching relationship?
- What do we need to discuss in order to work well together?
- How can we maximize our coaching relationship?

Rapport and mutual respect established

- How could we begin the process of getting to know each other better?
- Help me understand who you are. Examples: interests, gifts, personality, strengths, ministry calling, family, etc.
- Tell me about your spiritual journey. How would you describe your relationship with God right now?
- What wins can we celebrate?
- How are you doing personally? Your family? Other significant relationships?

Trusting relationship begun

- What is working (or not working) in our coaching relationship?
- What would improve our coaching relationship?
- What issues are truly important to you right now?
- What obstacles or challenges are you facing?
- How can I be praying for you?

Coaching agenda and guidelines determined

- What are your overall goals for this coaching relationship?
- What do you believe needs to happen in order to make progress toward those goals?
- What guidelines will we embrace for our coaching relationship?

NOTES

REFLECT

DISCOVER AND EXPLORE KEY ISSUES

The reflect phase of the coaching process focuses on the situation at hand. Attention is focused on gaining a clear understanding of the factors contributing to a problem, relationship, or issue. This careful reflection then sets the stage for designing action plans.

Coaches provide probing questions to help their leaders analyze the situation. Leaders gain clarity through understanding the key issues and categorizing them into themes.

A thorough diagnosis provides accurate information for goal setting. During this phase the coach is PROBING on several fronts to gain discernment in a given context, e.g. the health of a congregation, philosophy of ministry, conflict, etc. Any data retrieved must be succinctly identified before advancing to the next phase.

Key actions in the REFLECT phase:

Deeper understanding of key issues gained

Issues sorted by importance/urgency

Priority issues identified and agreed upon

Commitment to address issues obtained

DEEPER UNDERSTANDING OF KEY ISSUES GAINED

REFLECT

- A coach must ask probing questions to isolate the core issues contributing to the situation. Additional data gathered by interviewing other people involved will further crystallize the issues, giving the leader a firm grasp on the situation. Thorough diagnosis ultimately helps clarify vision, values, and mission.

- A coach brings an objective perspective leaders sometimes lack. Coaches can help leaders reach a greater understanding through identifying key issues contributing to the situation, problem, or challenge the leader is facing. In certain situations (e.g. church health, conflict, and leadership styles), inventories can also be helpful tools.

Reflection Questions

1. How well do you facilitate the discovery process through the use of probing questions?

2. What strategies do you employ to avoid simply "telling" people your solutions?

3. What are some powerful questions you can ask to help people clearly analyze their situation and discover key issues?

ISSUES SORTED BY IMPORTANCE/URGENCY

- Prioritizing key issues and themes will further advance the understanding of the leader. Be sure to distinguish between issues that are truly important and those that are merely urgent. Urgent issues are those that require immediate attention. Important issues contribute to your mission, values, and priority goals.

- Coaches are often tempted to set priorities for those they coach. Resist that temptation. When leaders identify their own goals, they own them. The outcome is a significantly higher degree of commitment.

- Feedback from others outside the coaching relationship can provide confirmation or additional input. A thorough assessment leads to a logical prioritization of the key themes and issues.

Reflection Questions

1. Define the difference between important and urgent. Give examples from your own life and ministry.

2. What methods can you use to guide the person you are coaching through the process of sorting out his/her issues according to priority?

PRIORITY ISSUES IDENTIFIED AND AGREED UPON

- Discerning priorities is a spiritual process. Encourage the person you are coaching to listen to the guidance of the Holy Spirit and the community of faith when selecting priorities.
- Effective coaches help leaders identify the other people who also need to embrace the priority issues. Without the concurrence and support of others, implementation can often be hindered significantly.
- Developing a strategy to obtain ownership of the priority issues may need to be included in the action plan during the refocus phase.

Reflection Questions

1. What coaching questions help people clarify and agree upon priority issues?

2. If you disagree with the person you are coaching regarding their assessment of needs and determination of goals, how will you proceed?

3. How can you help the people you are coaching determine who else needs to embrace the priorities identified?

REFLECT

COMMITMENT TO ADDRESS ISSUES OBTAINED

- What are you willing to sacrifice in order to reach your goals? That is the true test of commitment. At this point, the leader must take ownership and commit to the process if they are to progress toward the stated goals. Asking a simple question like "How committed are you?" can uncover deeper issues that may need to be addressed.

- Essential issues include: accountability structures, clarified expectations, attitudes, emotions, and next steps. Whether or not the leader follows through on taking the next step will be a significant indicator of commitment level and ownership.

Reflection Questions

1. How do you personally cultivate commitment?

2. Think about a time when you personally lacked the necessary commitment to accomplish a goal. What was missing? What was needed?

3. How can you help those you coach evaluate and strengthen their commitment to follow through on priority issues they have identified?

WHAT GOD HAS CALLED YOU TO DO

List your top three spiritual gifts:

List below the three or four ministry activities you enjoy most and feel most effective in (i.e., leadership, teaching, evangelism, administration, etc.). List in descending order:

If you knew you could not fail, what would you do for the glory of God?

In view of the above information, plus input from others, describe what you believe God has called you to do.

PRIORITY CLARIFICATION

What are the few important things, which if done with excellence, would really make a difference in your life and/or ministry?

Which one needs your attention now?

What is your role and/or contribution to make this happen?

What will you stop doing in order to make this a priority?

BALANCING PERSONAL ROLES AND PRIORITIES

With your calendar in hand, list all the activities you were involved in during the last 30 days according to the role that best defines each activity. List the amount of time each activity took, and evaluate your effectiveness on a scale of 1 to 5.

Role	Activities	Time	Effectiveness low high
	•		1 2 3 4 5
	•		1 2 3 4 5
	•		1 2 3 4 5
	•		1 2 3 4 5
	•		1 2 3 4 5
	•		1 2 3 4 5
	•		1 2 3 4 5
	•		1 2 3 4 5
	•		1 2 3 4 5
	•		1 2 3 4 5
		Total time given to role:	

Role	Activities	Time	Effectiveness low high
	•		1 2 3 4 5
	•		1 2 3 4 5
	•		1 2 3 4 5
	•		1 2 3 4 5
	•		1 2 3 4 5
	•		1 2 3 4 5
	•		1 2 3 4 5
	•		1 2 3 4 5
	•		1 2 3 4 5
	•		1 2 3 4 5
		Total time given to role:	

Role	Activities	Time	Effectiveness low high
	•		1 2 3 4 5
	•		1 2 3 4 5
	•		1 2 3 4 5
	•		1 2 3 4 5
	•		1 2 3 4 5
	•		1 2 3 4 5
	•		1 2 3 4 5
	•		1 2 3 4 5
	•		1 2 3 4 5
	•		1 2 3 4 5
	Total time given to role:		

Role	Activities	Time	Effectiveness low high
	•		1 2 3 4 5
	•		1 2 3 4 5
	•		1 2 3 4 5
	•		1 2 3 4 5
	•		1 2 3 4 5
	•		1 2 3 4 5
	•		1 2 3 4 5
	•		1 2 3 4 5
	•		1 2 3 4 5
	•		1 2 3 4 5
	Total time given to role:		

Role	Activities	Time	Effectiveness low high
	•		1 2 3 4 5
	•		1 2 3 4 5
	•		1 2 3 4 5
	•		1 2 3 4 5
	•		1 2 3 4 5
	•		1 2 3 4 5
	•		1 2 3 4 5
	•		1 2 3 4 5
	•		1 2 3 4 5
	•		1 2 3 4 5
	Total time given to role:		

Reflection

1. What role(s) do you need to invest more time in?

2. Cross out activities you could delete and no one would notice.

3. Cross out activities you could delegate effectively and list the activity below with the name of the person you can delegate it to.

Check when delegated		Activity	I can delegate to:	Target date
	☐			
	☐			
	☐			
	☐			
	☐			
	☐			

MINISTRY EVALUATION

Instructions:

1. Label each bar in the graph with one of your ministry responsibilities. Up to ten areas can be identified. For example: training, shepherding, teaching, leadership development, counseling, budgeting, etc.
2. On a scale of 1-10, draw a bar graph to show your level of satisfaction for each responsibility.
3. Based on your assessment, what area(s) do you want to address now?

Responsibility	1	2	3	4	5	6	7	8	9	10

Area of Responsibility	What needs to change?

UNDERSTANDING KEY ISSUES

Strengths What is working well?	Weaknesses What is missing or needs improvement?
Opportunities What possibilities do you see?	Threats What obstacles have you identified?

Describe accurately your current reality:

POWERFUL QUESTIONS

Reflect Checklist

Deeper understanding of key issues gained

- What has God called you to do?
- What are your hopes and dreams?
  (personal, family, ministry, school, work, etc.)
- Which of your responsibilities are you handling well?
  Which ones need attention?
- What obstacles are you facing?
- What opportunities do you see?

Issues sorted by importance/urgency

- Brainstorm a list of possible goals.
- What's really important?
- What's urgent but not important?
- Which issues feel most pressing to you right now?
- If you could improve just one area of your life or ministry, what would it be?

Priority issues identified and agreed upon

- Where do you want to go?
- What priorities will you focus on?
- How strongly do these priorities connect with your values?
- Who needs to embrace these priorities?
- What changes are needed to obtain concurrence?
- How will you cultivate agreement on the priorities?

Commitment to address issues obtained

- How committed are you?
- What are you willing to endure?
- What will you stop doing to free up time and energy?
- What will you start doing to focus your efforts?
- What will you continue doing?
- Who can help encourage and assist you?
- What accountability structures will help you maintain focus?

NOTES

NOTES

REFOCUS

Determine priorities and action steps

The refocus phase of the coaching process points to the future. After gathering information during the reflect phase, the focus now shifts to vision, values, and goals. The resulting action plan advances the personal and ministry development of the leader.

Envisioning the future from God's perspective plays a central role in the coaching process. And making that future a reality requires planning. Brainstorming options, prioritizing action plans, and assigning dates are all steps in the planning process. The end result is an action plan that helps the leader fulfill God's purposes in their life and ministry.

Concentrate on identifying the really important issues— the things that will make the greatest impact. During this phase the coach is CHALLENGING to help clarify how and when the action plan will be implemented. To a great extent, a solid action plan determines the success of the coaching relationship.

Key actions in the REFOCUS phase:

Vision clarified

Possible solutions brainstormed

Decisions made according to priorities

Commitment to action confirmed

Change dynamics considered

Action steps determined and time line developed

Accountability structure agreed upon

VISION CLARIFIED

- Vision provides a clear picture of a preferred future according to God's will for an individual, team, church, or organization. Vision catches a glimpse of reality from God's perspective and seeks his specific assignment. Vision inspires, challenges and empowers us; it clarifies our purpose and direction. Ultimately, vision bridges the present and the future in a way that sets standards of excellence flowing out of God's redemptive purposes.

- Remember that the function of the coach is to help people discover God's agenda for their life and ministry, then find ways to cooperate with that agenda. Asking probing questions to evaluate the critical components of a vision and their practicality is an important role for the coach. Excellent coaches find creative approaches to facilitate the visioning process of others.

Reflection Questions

1. How do you cultivate vision from God?

2. How does the visioning process involve God and other people?

3. What coaching questions can help people focus their vision more clearly?

POSSIBLE SOLUTIONS BRAINSTORMED

- The art of coaching is knowing when to remain silent and when to speak. Excellent coaches help leaders exhaust all possibilities before offering their own thoughts. The goal for the coach is to be a catalyst to creativity rather than to offer expert advice.

- Brainstorming is a powerful process guided by one core principle: "No idea is a dumb idea." Effective brainstorming allows a leader to generate as many ideas as possible that contribute toward a solution, a goal, or a vision.

- Brainstorming helps leaders think beyond the limitations of the present and dream. Its benefits cannot be overstated.

Reflection Questions

1. What lessons have you learned from your brainstorming experiences?

2. How can you spark greater creativity when brainstorming with those you coach?

DECISIONS MADE ACCORDING TO PRIORITIES

- Helping people in the decision-making process is a key micro-skill of excellent coaches. Ask the leader your are coaching how their goals line up with their expressed values. That exercise alone will begin to clarify their thinking and help them set priorities.

- Coaches can also help tackle difficult issues by breaking them down into several smaller, more manageable parts. Once those pieces are identified, it is often easier to see what will be required for successful resolution, streamlining the decision-making process.

- When divergent opinions and perspectives exist, coaches can help people dialogue and resolve differences. An excellent coach can facilitate without taking over and undermining a sense of ownership. Such a posture ensures that the leader remains at the center of the coaching relationship.

Reflection Questions

1. How do you personally measure the alignment between decisions you make and your values?

2. How will you respond if the person you are coaching makes decisions that are unwise in your opinion?

3. Reflect on the goals of the person you are coaching. How can you help make the attainment of those goals more manageable?

COMMITMENT TO ACTION CONFIRMED

- Confirming the commitment of the leader is vital to the successful implementation of an action plan. Without commitment, even the best plans will come to nothing.

- Excellent coaches ask probing questions to help leaders understand the action necessary for success. Concrete expectations for improvement are important to identify so everyone is on the same page. A clear understanding of these expectations will determine the kind of action required.

- Once the action is identified then a commitment must be made to act.

Reflection Questions

1. How can you help others confirm and strengthen their commitment to action?

2. What are some ways to help others design their own support system and accountability structures?

CHANGE DYNAMICS CONSIDERED

- Coaching is all about change for leaders and their teams— and change can be difficult to deal with, even positive change. Change dynamics must be considered.

- Five key aspects of change dynamics are identifying obstacles, preparing people for change, acknowledging both positive and negative potential impact, compensating for blind spots, and motivating people towards vision.

- Excellent coaches help leaders anticipate and deal with resistance. Coaches can help leaders anticipate and navigate change by drawing out insights through asking probing questions. Realizing personal costs to those involved, whether direct or indirect, can bring about an awareness of the risks and clarity regarding the best course of action.

Reflection Questions

1. When dealing with change, what are some of the best practices that you have observed or experienced?

2. How can you help the person you are coaching prepare himself/herself and others for change?

REFOCUS

ACTION STEPS DETERMINED AND TIME LINE DEVELOPED

- Excellent coaches guide people in developing a coherent, organized plan of action that suits that leader's unique style. One common challenge is determining ways to keep the planning process concrete and practical.

- A good action plan clarifies:

  Who? What? How? When? Cost?

- Once measurable goals have been agreed upon, realistic steps to reach those goals should be identified. Defining a reasonable time line for each goal is the final, critical step to determining action steps.

Reflection Questions

1. How will you keep the planning process concrete and practical?

2. Given the unique style of the person you are coaching, how can you best help them develop a coherent, organized plan of action?

ACCOUNTABILITY STRUCTURE AGREED UPON

- Accountability is designed to ensure the completion of action plans. The accountability you agree upon should address the frequency, content, and duration of your coaching relationship. This single micro-skill can mean the difference between a successful coaching process and failure.

- Don't always assume that you as the coach need to serve as the primary accountability person. Instead, ask: "Who can help you stay on track?"

SHARPENING YOUR VISION

Prayerfully develop 3 to 5 vision statements that establish a God-given direction consistent with your values and mission.

What?	By when?

Identify your key result areas. How will you measure your effectiveness?

Key Result Areas	Measurement

ACTION PLANNER

1. Clarify your goal:

Specific

Measurable

Achievable

Related to your vision

Timeframe

2. Determine your action steps

Who?	What?	How?	When?	Cost?

3. Complete reality checks

- What important steps are missing?

- How could your plan be more effective?

- How and when will you evaluate your progress?

CHANGE GUIDE

1. How will you free up time and energy to focus on the change process?

2. Who are the key people who can work with you to facilitate the change process?

3. Who are the key influencers who need to embrace the vision and/or be included in the discussion/planning process?

4. What permissions need to be secured? From whom?

CHANGE GUIDE

1. Who are the people/groups most affected by the proposed changes? What impact will each face?

You Personally

Your Family

Ministries

Others

2. What can you do to help people embrace the change?

3. How will you strengthen relationships during the change process?

POWERFUL QUESTIONS

Refocus Checklist

Vision clarified

- If you knew that you could not fail, what would you do for the glory of God and the growth of his kingdom?
- Describe your ideal vision. What opportunities do you see?
- What obstacles could prevent you from realizing your vision?
- If God could have his way, how would your life or ministry be different 10 years from now?
- What kind of help do you need in clarifying your vision?
- What components of your vision need clarification?

Possible solutions brainstormed

- What would you like to see happen in a given situation?
- What are possible ways to get there?
- How have other people handled similar situations?
- What unconventional or creative approaches could be pursued?

Decisions made according to priorities

- What decisions need to be made?
- What principles will guide your decision making process?
- After evaluating your brainstorming, examine the reasons why
- You have ruled out certain options. How valid are those reasons?
- Of all the possibilities you have come up with, which might be best? How did you arrive at that conclusion?
- What issue feels like the most difficult to tackle? How might you be able to break that issue down into several smaller, more manageable parts?

Commitment to action confirmed

- What commitment to action are you willing to make?
- What are you willing to endure to see your vision become a reality?
- What are your next steps?

Change dynamics considered

- How do you need to change personally?
- What personal obstacles do you need to overcome?
- Who else will be affected by your proposed course of action?
- What resistance do you expect to the changes you will be making? How will you handle that resistance?
- How will you encourage and motivate others to share your vision and direction?

Action steps determined and time line developed

- What are your immediate, short-term, and long-term plans?
- What specific initiatives could help you accomplish your goals?
- What feedback would be helpful from others? How will you obtain that input?
- What specific measurable steps will you take?
- When will you take those steps?
- What tasks can you delegate to others?
- Given your current plan of action, what is the worst-case scenario of what could happen? What is the best-case scenario?
- What questions can you ask of your plan to test its soundness?

Accountability structure agreed upon

- How will you measure your progress?
- Who can help you stay on track?
- What accountability structures will you establish?
- How will you commit to moving forward toward the fulfillment of your goals?
- How would you like to be held accountable?

NOTES

RESOURCE

PROVIDE SUPPORT AND ENCOURAGEMENT

During the resource phase, the coach will help the leader maintain a clear focus of the vision while giving attention to the resource needs of the person being coached. The primary task of the coach is to FACILITATE the brainstorming, assessing, and identifying of needed resources throughout implementation.

Changes in a situation means changes in resources; excellent coaches help leaders adapt accordingly.

Change is a constant in ministry. Coaches help people consider the implications when introducing, adapting, or replacing resources. Anticipating the repercussions when changes are made in a new or existing project can help the person you are coaching avoid setbacks and maximize the opportunity.

As effective resources are identified and utilized, the person being coached will be in a better position to carry out the next steps in their action plan. The right resource applied in the right way will have a tremendous impact on a ministry. Ample time and attention must be given to the resource phase in the coaching process.

Key actions in the RESOURCE phase:

Existing resources assessed

All resource needs brainstormed

New resource(s) identified to accomplish goals

Where and how to find new resources determined

Role of coach clarified and confirmed

EXISTING RESOURCES ASSESSED

- Coaches that help those they coach routinely and intentionally assess existing resources increase the likelihood of success.

- Excellent coaches intentionally help people determine whether the resources being used are accomplishing their intended purpose. Resources that are not effective should be modified or replaced.

- Keep in mind that if plans are made according to the will of God, then the resources necessary to carry out that plan will be available or can be discovered.

Reflection Questions

1. How have you creatively utilized existing resources to accomplish a goal that seemed at first overwhelming?

2. What coaching questions could help others assess their resources effectively?

RESOURCE

ALL RESOURCE NEEDS BRAINSTORMED

- Resources can range from people, money, and time to ministry tools, programs, and books. The person you are coaching and the context they minister in dictate what resources are required. Excellent coaches help people they coach discover their resourcing options by brainstorming possibilities.

- Make sure that you begin with existing resources. People often overlook the powerful assets that they already have available. Then continue the brainstorming to think creatively about other resources that would be helpful during implementation.

- The goal of brainstorming is to exhaust all possible resource options. Many times just when the person you are coaching believes they have exhausted all of their options, they are actually on the brink of making a discovery. It is at this juncture excellent coaches ask for "just five more ideas." These ideas are sometimes what make the difference between a good solution and the best solution.

Reflection Questions

1. How can you apply the principle of interdependence to discover potential resources?

2. What questions can you ask that will probe, challenge and advance the thinking of the person you are coaching to pin- point their resourcing needs?

NEW RESOURCE(S) IDENTIFIED TO ACCOMPLISH GOALS

- As action plans are implemented, new resources may need to be discovered to overcome challenges.
- Excellent coaches help those they coach identify new resources by asking questions to probe, challenge, and advance the thinking of the people they coach. You can also help people get connected to needed resources.

Reflection Questions

1. How can you increase your access to helpful resources? For yourself? For those you coach?

2. What questions can you ask that will stimulate creativity to discover new resources?

WHERE AND HOW TO FIND NEW RESOURCES DETERMINED

- Acquiring needed resources can sometimes be challenging. Where do you look? How do you proceed? The best place to start is with people and places that are familiar. Brainstorming is a good first step to unleash creativity.

- Make sure you first unpack the best thinking of the person you are coaching before contributing your own ideas. Then follow up with questions to develop specific action plans to obtain necessary resources. Excellent coaches seek to provide just the right amount of help— not too much or too little.

Reflection Questions

1. How have you creatively discovered new resources when initially you had no idea where to look?

2. Who are the best resource people in your area(s) of coaching? How can you establish or strengthen relationships with them?

ROLE OF COACH CLARIFIED AND CONFIRMED

- Excellent coaches clarify their role in the coaching relationship after identifying the resource needs of the person being coached. For example, if the complexity of a ministry situation increases, the coaching agenda and frequency of coaching appointments may change as well.

- Ask those you coach how you can be more helpful to them as they implement their action plans. Taking the time to evaluate and make adjustments can avoid the ambiguity that derails many coaching relationships.

Reflection Questions

1. How do you seek feedback from others so you can grow?

2. How have you identified personal blind spots?

3. How have you overcome weaknesses that have been pointed out to you?

4. What recent steps have you taken for self-development?

QUICK AND SIMPLE ASSET MAPPING

An asset is anything—time, gifts, talents, relationships, etc.—that might be useful in accomplishing what God has called you to do. Asset mapping is an easy and powerful way to organize those tools. You can use an asset map individually or with group.

To make your asset map, you'll need a few things for each participant:

- A stack of Post-It™ Notes (7-10 per person, minimum)
- A dark pen... Sharpies™ or similar is ideal
- Some wall or table space
- A minimum of 30 minutes

Asset-Mapping Process

The following steps are designed to be followed in one session and will help you design your asset map. The pieces of the process follow this format:

1. **Identify your assets (Spend a few minutes coming up with the particular assets you have available to you.)**
   - Select an area of focus.
   - Write down one asset per Post-It™ note.
   - Don't overlook assets.
   - Display each asset.

2. **Link what you've got. (Assets will fit together to form the basis of a plan to advance your project. You'll probably have more assets than you need and you'll find it easy to come up with multiple plans.)**
   - Connect several assets.
   - Brainstorm possible actions.
   - Connect to other assets.
   - Give the action a name.

3. **Choose your best option(s). (After looking at all of your options for moving forward, choose which option(s) you'll pursue.)**
    - Design an action that helps you accomplish your project.
    - Get buy-in.
    - Make a work plan.

4. **Repeat!**

Based on work from *The Great Permission* by Laurel Hensel & Bob Sitze (Augsburg Fortress, 2002) and The Power of Asset *Mapping: How Your Congregation Can Act on Its Gifts* by Luther Snow (Alban Institute, 2004)

POWERFUL QUESTIONS

Resource Checklist

Existing resources assessed

- What's helpful?
- What's not as helpful?
- What's missing?
- What's confused?
- What's needed?

All resource needs brainstormed

- What assets do you already have?
- What resources have you heard others recommend?
- Who do you know that would know about helpful resources?
- What other resources might be needed to implement your plans?
- How can you generate more possibilities?

New resources identified to accomplish goals

- What resources do you need to implement your action plans?
- What resources are you aware of that could be helpful in this situation?
- What changes can you make to utilize your existing resources more effectively?
- What steps can you take to discover new resources?
- What resources have other people recommended?

Where and how to find new resources determined

- Who do you know that has gone through a similar experience?
- What resources have other people used?
- What resources have other people recommended?
- Where can you go to find what you need?

Role of coach clarified and confirmed

- In what ways can I encourage you?
- How can I be a more helpful resource to you?
- When will we have our next coaching appointment? How long should we meet?
- What changes could we make to increase the effectiveness of our coaching relationship?

NOTES

NOTES

REVIEW

EVALUATE, CELEBRATE AND REVISE PLANS

The review phase of the coaching process allows time for reflection. At this point, the coach provides the leader with an opportunity to assess what's happened so far, extract principles, and learn from the experience.

Evaluation in some form is essential after implementing an action plan—it fosters learning, challenge, and accountability. The evaluation should include an assessment of the coaching relationship as well as a discussion of future projects.

Remember that coaching is a discovery process. The primary task of the coach is SUMMARIZING to identify key discoveries. After bringing a sense of closure, the coaching relationship is then either terminated or renewed, depending on the leader's goals. A healthy review phase provides a sense of fulfillment and leaves the leader wanting more.

Key actions in the Review phase:

Action plan and process evaluated
Progress celebrated
Learning maximized
Mid-course corrections made
New projects identified
Coaching relationship evaluated

ACTION PLAN AND PROCESS EVALUATED

- Evaluation occurs throughout the implementation process and upon completion of the project. Excellent coaches bring about awareness through the use of probing, open-ended questions.

- During implementation, the action plan is evaluated checking for progress towards the completion of goals. The coach's role is to keep the leader focused on the plan even when resistance and unresolved conflicts are revealed. A coach can also help by bringing certain matters to the attention of the leader.

- Effective coaches also seek feedback from those they coach to determine how the coaching process helped them accomplish their goals.

Reflection Questions

1. In what ways have you evaluated progress on personal project(s) you have undertaken?

2. How could you improve your evaluation process on future projects?

3. How well are you able to keep to your priorities clear during the implementation process? What are some obstacles that might be sidetracking you?

PROGRESS CELEBRATED

- The progress leaders make affords opportunities for celebration. Excellent coaches take the initiative to celebrate. A key to meaningful celebration is discovering ways to tap into the emotions of those you coach. What works for one person may not work for another. Learn how to adapt to the personalities and styles of those you coach.

- Celebrations should be intentional and meaningful. It's easy to let opportunities fall by the wayside, and having specific plans for providing encouragement along the way helps intentionalize ways to celebrate progress. When a milestone has been reached, the coach may provide the leader with a special memento to commemorate the event.

Reflection Questions

1. How intentional are you in celebrating little wins along the way?

2. What are some ways you have previously celebrated progress? How could these times have been more meaningful?

LEARNING MAXIMIZED

- Coaches provide those they coach with a disciplined pause in their activity to review the work of God in their lives and ministries. Help those you coach reflect after they have executed an action step and before they move on to the next. By learning from their experience, people can become more fruitful.

- There are three points at which people are generally most receptive to reflection and learning. The first is at the conclusion of their action plan when they have celebrated their success. The second is when they have experienced a failure. The third is at the conclusion of a coaching appointment. Open-ended questions can open the door to new realizations for those you coach.

- Key insights made during a reflection exercise of this nature can accomplish much more than receiving the information from an outside, secondary source. When lessons are learned from real experience, the person who makes the discovery will have greater understanding and ownership. Discoveries made at this level foster the development of wisdom.

Reflection Questions

1. What are you learning from your coaching experience?

2. How can you cultivate disciplines to increase wisdom?

3. What questions could you ask to facilitate the learning of those you coach?

MID-COURSE CORRECTIONS MADE

- Even the best plans need to be modified to maximize results. When implementing change, adjustments will often be necessary.

- Mid-course corrections should be considered when an action plan is failing to achieve its intended purpose. Excellent coaches are creative and can help leaders design alternative approaches. By asking probing questions and assessing progress throughout implementation, leaders will see more effective ways to accomplish their goals.

Reflection Questions

1. What adjustments need to be made in your coaching relationships?

2. How can you facilitate the process of helping others make mid-course corrections?

3. What questions can you ask to help people revise their plans?

NEW PROJECTS IDENTIFIED

- A review of the action plan may bring to light areas that need to be addressed or altered. In some cases, a new plan may need to be developed in order to strategically address those new initiatives.

- Excellent coaches help leaders consider the next steps in their personal development as well as in their ministries. New projects identified give focused attention for the future. Considering the future builds momentum for the next stage in the leader's development.

- Leaders will benefit greatly by the care and attention you give them in identifying future projects. Whether or not you will continue to be involved as their coach is irrelevant here, since your focus is on them and what God has for them in the future. Remember the overall aim of an excellent coach: to help others discover God's agenda for their life and ministry and find ways to cooperate with that agenda.

Reflection Questions

1. What new projects are you anticipating for the person you are coaching? How would he or she feel about those new projects?

2. What are some practical ways you can help the person you are coaching take on the challenges that lie ahead?

COACHING RELATIONSHIP EVALUATED

- The coaching relationship is first evaluated to determine if the expectations have been achieved. In addition to their self-assessment, the coach asks the leader to assess their performance in achieving the goals.
- Coaches learn and grow best through ongoing assessment. When issues surface during the coaching relationship, coaches can take action to address that area effectively and efficiently.
- Excellent coaches seek to gain an accurate assessment of the relationship as a whole; they assess its quality regularly to determine how it is progressing. If this dimension is ignored the leader may drift and the coach may be the last to realize the relationship has come to a premature end. One area to test is the satisfaction level of leaders regarding their progress towards goals they established.
- The conclusion of the process presents another opportunity to evaluate. This window provides a tremendous time for reflection and culmination, allowing leaders to give thoughtful feedback, celebrate, and bring closure in an affirming manner. Capturing these insights at this opportune moment will give the coach a reality check and contribute to their growth.

Reflection Questions

1. How are your coaching relationships progressing?

2. What barriers prevent you from talking openly with the person you are coaching as you evaluate your mutual progress?

REVIEW

3. How has your current coaching relationship been different than others you have been involved in? To what degree are those differences reproducible?

4. What things would you do differently if you had it to do over again?

ACTION PLAN EVALUATION

Observations and Reflection

- Expected results (goals):

- Significant "wins":

- Obstacles encountered:

- Lessons learned:

- Changes needed:

- Next steps:

COACHING PROCESS EVALUATION

RELATE– Establish coaching relationship and agenda	
AFFIRMATIONS	IMPROVEMENTS
REFLECT– Discover and explore key issues	
AFFIRMATIONS	IMPROVEMENTS
REFOCUS– Determine priorities and action steps	
AFFIRMATIONS	IMPROVEMENTS
RESOURCE– Provide support and encouragement	
AFFIRMATIONS	IMPROVEMENTS
REVIEW– Evaluate, celebrate and revise plans	
AFFIRMATIONS	IMPROVEMENTS

POWERFUL QUESTIONS

Review Checklist

Action plan and process evaluated

- What progress have you made on your action plans?
- To what degree have you met your own expectations and hopes?
- What has not gone as well as expected?
- What has disappointed you in the implementation process?
- What feedback have you received from others outside our coaching relationship?
- What long-term benefits have you begun to realize?

Progress celebrated

- What's something you are excited about?
- What milestones have you accomplished?
- What answers to prayer have you received?
- Where do you see God working in your life?
- How has God been faithful?
- How have you celebrated your progress?
- What outside evidence validates the efforts you have put forth? (accomplishments, the comments of others, etc.)

Learning maximized

- What are you learning from your experience?
- How could you increase your learning in this situation?
- What is one insight you have gained from our time together?

Mid-course corrections made

- What adjustments need to be made to the action plan at this point?
- How will you carry out those adjustments?
- What are the specific tasks facing you right now that you consider incomplete?
- What would be the best way to address those tasks?
- What still needs to be accomplished?
- What specific actions need to be taken to address those issues?

New projects identified

- What additional ministry challenges lie ahead?
- Let's brainstorm a list of possible new projects.
- Which new projects would you like to tackle next?
- Which new projects feel most pressing? Which are more important?
- How can I best help you face these challenges?

Coaching relationship evaluated

- How do you feel this coaching relationship is progressing?
- In what ways has this coaching relationship met your expectations? In what ways has it not?
- What elements were most helpful to you?
- In what cases would you have liked to see me take a different approach? Elaborate.
- How would you evaluate your own role in the coaching relationship?
- How could our coaching relationship improve?
- What is next in our coaching relationship?

COACHING JOURNAL

Personalize and track your ongoing development as a coach. Record insights, design action plans, and index your favorite coaching questions. Intentionalize your personal development by periodically setting aside time to reflect and mine the wisdom from your coaching experience.

1. Insights I have gleaned from the coaching process:

	Lessons learned	Progress made
Relate		
Reflect		
Refocus		
Resource		
Review		

2. Which phase do I need to sharpen in my coaching process?

3. What specific improvements need to be made?

ACTION PLAN TO ADDRESS THIS PHASE

What	How	When

1. Resources I need to implement my action plan (example: coach mentor, seminars, books, etc.):

2. Powerful coaching questions I have used and want to remember.

- Relate:
- Reflect:
- Refocus:
- Resource:
- Review:

3. Date and time I will review my coaching development.

   Date:______________Time:___________am/pm

NOTES

NOTES

AUTHOR BIOS

Dr. Robert E. Logan has over 40 years of ministry experience, including church planting, pastoring, consulting, coaching, and speaking. Having seen a great deal, Bob remains on the cutting edge of ministry through hands-on missional involvement. He counts it a privilege to walk alongside ministry leaders and help catalyze their ministries toward fulfilling the call God has placed on them, and he thrives in developing holistic and transformative resources that can easily be implemented in any context. Bob and his wife, Janet, live in Northern CA.

Dr. Gary B. Reinecke is the Executive Director of InFocus and trains leaders world-wide in the coaching process and skills. He has been coaching leaders for disciple-making, leadership development and church multiplication since 1988. Gary co-authored *Developing Coaching Excellence.* He received the designation of Master Certified Coach with the International Coach Federation in 2018. Gary and his wife, Gina, live in Southern CA.

SUGGESTED RESOURCES

Suggested Coaching Resources

Coaching 101: Discover the Power of Coaching - The book that started it all! Companion resource to the *Coaching 101 Handbook*, *Coaching 101* lays out the basic essentials of the coaching process, including the 5 Rs. If you want to launch your journey as a coach, this is the place to start. Also available in Spanish, Portuguese, French, Korean, Czech, Italian, and Russian. Learn more by visiting: https://loganleadership.com/C101

Becoming Barnabas - This short book sets forth the biblical basis for coaching-- tied to the story of Barnabas-- and describes how it can transform your ministry through the everyday practice of basic coaching skills by laypeople and clergy alike. Learn more by visiting: https://loganleadership.com/BB

Other resources you may find helpful

Leadership Difference - A book providing practical guidance on developing essential leadership skills within a coaching paradigm. To learn more or purchase this resource visit: https://loganleadership.com/LD

Leadership Skills Guides- Easy to use and highly customizable, these coaching guides help you foster 37 essential leadership skills in your existing and developing leaders. To learn more and purchase this downloadable resource visit: https://loganleadership.com/LSG

Leadership Multiplication Pathway- A visual storyboard designed to give you a systemic and comprehensive process for developing more and better leaders within your ministry. To learn more and purchase this downloadable resource visit: https://loganleadership.com/LMP

Printed by Amazon Italia Logistica S.r.l.
Torrazza Piemonte (TO), Italy

11472010R00055